WORLD WAR II CHRONICLES

THE WAR AT HOME

DWIGHT JON ZIMMERMAN,
MILITARY HISTORY CONSULTANT

BY JULIE KLAM

Published by Smart Apple Media, 1980 Lookout Drive, North Mankato, Minnesota 56003

Produced by Byron Preiss Visual Publications, Inc.

Library of Congress Cataloging-in-Publication Data

Klam, Julie.

The war at home / by Julie Klam.

v. cm. — (World War II chronicles; bk. 4)

Contents: Americans answer the call: war bonds — Victory gardens — Collections and recycling — Ration books — Civil Defense: air
raid wardens — Traveling here and abroad: draft and domestic travel — Japanese relocation centers — Jim Crow here and abroad —
Women in the war: Rosie the Riveter — Women journalists — Women in the ranks — How people got the news: newspapers,
newsreels, radio — Propaganda — Victory.

ISBN 1-58340-190-3

1. World War, 1939-1945—United States—Juvenile literature. 2. United States—History—1933-1945—Juvenile literature. [1. World
War, 1939-1945—United States. 2. United States—History—1933-1945.] I. Title.

D769 .K53 2002

940.53'73—dc21   2002017649

First Edition

2 4 6 8 9 7 5 3 1

CONTENTS:

INTRODUCTION

✝ (opposite): Adolf Hitler addresses the Reichstag.

World War II was the greatest conflict of the 20th century. Fought on every continent except Antarctica and across every ocean, it was truly a "world war." Like many other wars, over time it evolved. Modern technology and strategic advancements changed the rules of combat forever, allowing for widespread attacks from the air, the ground, and the sea.

For the Chinese, the war began in 1931, when Japan invaded northeastern China. When Germany invaded Poland in 1939, Europeans were dragged into the fray. Americans did not enter World War II until December 7, 1941, when Japan attacked Pearl Harbor, Hawaii.

World War II pitted two sides against each other, the Axis powers and the Allied countries. The main Axis nations were Germany, Japan, and Italy. The Axis powers were led by Chancellor Adolf Hitler, the head of the Nazi Party in Germany; Premier Benito Mussolini, the head of the Fascists in Italy; and Japan's Emperor Hirohito and the military government headed by Prime Minister Hideki Tojo. The Allies included Britain, France, the Soviet Union, China, and the United States. The leaders of the Allies were Britain's Prime

✝ Benito Mussolini

✝ Hirohito

✠ Winston Churchill

Minister Winston Churchill, who had replaced Neville Chamberlain in 1940; General Charles de Gaulle of France; the Soviet Union's Marshal Josef Stalin; China's Generalissimo Chiang Kai-shek; and Franklin Delano Roosevelt, the president of the United States. The two sides clashed primarily in the Pacific Ocean and Asia, which Japan sought to control, and in the Atlantic Ocean, Europe, and North Africa, where Germany and Italy were trying to take over.

World War II finally ended in 1945, first in Europe on May 8, with Germany's total capitulation. Then, on September 2, the Japanese signed the document for their unconditional surrender after the United States had dropped two atomic bombs on Japan. World War II left 50 million people dead and millions of others wounded, both physically and mentally.

The war encompassed the feats of extraordinary heroes and the worst villains imaginable, with thrilling triumphs and heartrending tragedies. *The War at Home* details how American civilians supported the efforts of their troops overseas.

✠ Charles de Gaulle

⊦ Josef Stalin

⊦ Chiang Kai-shek

⊦ (right): Franklin Delano Roosevelt

Map of German Conquests

- Germany (1939)
- Axis Occupied Territory (1942)
- Italy and Its Territories
- Treaty with Axis
- Allied Powers
- Allied Protectorates
- Neutral Countries
- Vichy France and Territories

NORWAY

FINLAND

SWEDEN

North Sea

ESTONIA

Baltic Sea

LATVIA

IRELAND

UNITED KINGDOM

DENMARK

LITHUANIA

UNION OF SOVIET SOCIALIST REPUBLICS

EAST PRUSSIA

THE NETHERLANDS

BELGIUM

GERMANY

POLAND

Atlantic Ocean

LUXEMBOURG

FRANCE

SLOVAKIA

SWITZERLAND

HUNGARY

VICHY FRANCE

ROMANIA

Black Sea

YUGOSLAVIA

PORTUGAL

ITALY

Adriatic Sea

BULGARIA

SPAIN

ALBANIA

TURKEY

SPANISH MOROCCO

GREECE

SYRIA

MOROCCO

Mediterranean Sea

IRAQ

PALESTINE

TUNISIA

TRANS-JORDAN

ALGERIA

EGYPT

SAUDI ARABIA

LIBYA

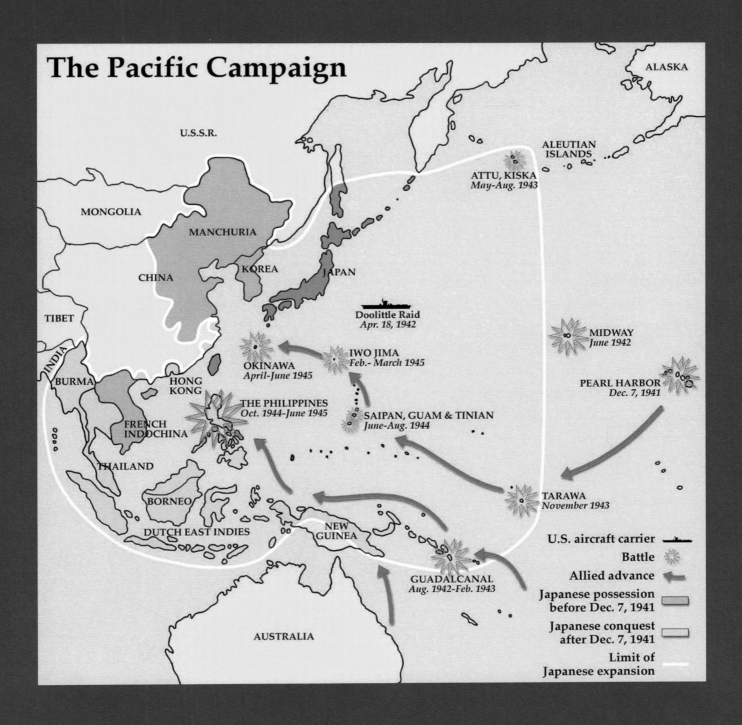

The Pacific Campaign

ALASKA

U.S.S.R.

ALEUTIAN ISLANDS

ATTU, KISKA
May-Aug. 1943

MONGOLIA

MANCHURIA

KOREA

CHINA

JAPAN

Doolittle Raid
Apr. 18, 1942

MIDWAY
June 1942

TIBET

OKINAWA
April-June 1945

IWO JIMA
Feb.- March 1945

PEARL HARBOR
Dec. 7, 1941

INDIA

BURMA

HONG KONG

THE PHILIPPINES
Oct. 1944-June 1945

SAIPAN, GUAM & TINIAN
June-Aug. 1944

FRENCH INDOCHINA

THAILAND

BORNEO

TARAWA
November 1943

DUTCH EAST INDIES

NEW GUINEA

AUSTRALIA

GUADALCANAL
Aug. 1942-Feb. 1943

U.S. aircraft carrier

Battle

Allied advance

Japanese possession
before Dec. 7, 1941

Japanese conquest
after Dec. 7, 1941

Limit of
Japanese expansion

AMERICA ANSWERS THE CALL: WAR BONDS

After the Japanese attack on Pearl Harbor on December 7, 1941, the United States entered the war politically, militarily, and spiritually. Life as Americans knew it would never be the same. Surprisingly, many of the changes were positive.

During the 1930s, America, like much of the rest of the world, suffered from an economic depression. People found themselves jobless, homeless, and profoundly hopeless. After America entered the war, a booming new industry revitalized the nation: war. The unemployment rate dropped from 25 percent to 1 percent, and per capita income doubled. Because most of the goods produced were for the war, there weren't many new products for the average person to buy, so personal savings increased during this time, too. In 1939, private Americans' savings added up to $2.6 billion; in 1944, it was $29.6 billion. One of the primary places they put their savings was war bonds.

A bond is a financial agreement that allows an issuer—in this case the U.S. government—to borrow money from a bond buyer, with the understanding that the money will be paid back with interest at an agreed-upon time. The U.S. Treasury began issuing what it called Series E Savings Bonds in May 1941 to help pay for the war efforts. After Pearl Harbor, the bonds became known as war bonds or victory bonds. They

Advertising was used to encourage Americans to purchase war bonds.

FINAL MORNING EXTRA
San Francisco Chronicle

U.S. AT WAR!
Japs Bomb Hawaii, Philippines, Invade Thailand, Malaya; U.S. Battleships Claimed Sunk; FDR Talks to Congress Today!

⊢ A workman in Shasta County, California, reads about the Pearl Harbor attack on December 7, 1941.

were the same bonds with a patriotic label.

Even though the United States had issued bonds to help fund previous wars, bonds became something of a cultural phenomenon during World War II. The government raised more than $185 billion from war bonds from 1941 through 1945, with more than 85 million Americans purchasing them—more than half of the U.S. population at the time. Even children put dimes toward the bonds that would help the boys overseas.

VICTORY GARDENS

An unusual and highly successful public relations campaign was the government's request for Americans to plant "victory gardens." These were vegetable gardens that came in every shape and size and were used to promote self-reliance. In theory, if people grew their own vegetables, they would not depend so heavily on manufactured goods.

Nearly 20 million Americans, from the cities to the suburbs, worked the soil to raise food for their families. The gardens produced up to 40 percent of all the food that was consumed. These efforts freed up more supplies to be shipped to the troops overseas.

Posters advertising victory gardens showed happy homes with a mother in the garden or canning vegetables in the kitchen, her pigtailed daughter by her side saying, "We'll have lots to eat this winter, won't we, Mother?" Corporations and government agencies published booklets encouraging and teaching about the satisfaction of growing your own food. They taught the basics of gardening, including soil health, how and when to plant, how to take care of plants and ward off pests, and

Victory gardeners doing their part for the war effort in Forest Hills, New York, 1944.

suggested what vegetables to plant in what climates. Emphasis was placed on making the planting and harvesting a family or community effort. People began to see gardening as their patriotic duty.

However, when the fighting of World War II ended, so too did the government's call for people to produce their own food.

⊣ An example of the campaign props to grow your own victory garden.

COLLECTIONS AND RECYCLING

After the Japanese attack on Pearl Harbor in 1941, the U.S. government asked its citizens to undertake an ambitious recycling and salvaging campaign. Items requested during this time included aluminum, copper, tin, rubber, steel, and even cooking fat.

The reason for this call to recycle was not to help the environment but to aid the war effort. Although production facilities were in place to build airplanes, bombs, weaponry, and ships, the raw materials needed were not readily available. When Japan took over Southeast Asia, America lost a great supplier of rubber, among other materials. And military industries needed aluminum, rubber, and copper immediately.

Household appliances and metal office furniture such as desks, file cabinets, and chairs were salvaged for conversion. Metal furniture was replaced with wood substitutes. To conserve raw rubber, old tires were recycled and made into new tires. People collected everything from tin cans to chewing gum wrappers to milkweed, which was used for stuffing in life jackets.

With recycling and collecting, everyone from senior citizens to children could help the war effort. And the American people responded to the call. During one two-week period, the Boy Scouts of America collected 30 million pounds (13.5 million kg) of scrap rubber!

To keep U.S. supplies from running out during the war, some foods and gasoline were rationed. Each individual or family was allotted a limited amount of rationed items. To keep track of this, everyone was given a ration book every month, which contained a certain number of stamps based on the size of the family. Once the book was empty, a person had to make do until the end of the month. If he needed more sugar, he'd have to either borrow it from a friend or wait.

By 1943, foods that came under rationing included butter, sugar, coffee, dairy products, and meat. Each item was assigned a certain number of ration points in addition to its monetary price. Shoppers would have to pay and give stamps, and if a stamp had a higher value than an item, tokens were given as change. But shoppers could earn extra stamps by turning in their meat drippings and other fats, which, believe it or not, would be put toward making bombs.

Gasoline for use in civilian cars was also rationed, and people were given stamps based on their need to drive. People with driving essential to their profession, such as doctors, were given more gas stamps, and nonessential drivers were limited to only three gallons (11.4 l) a week. During the war, drivers drove very slowly to conserve both tire rubber and gas—no one wanted to run out of gas without the ration stamps to refill his tank.

 Americans line up for ration books in March 1943.

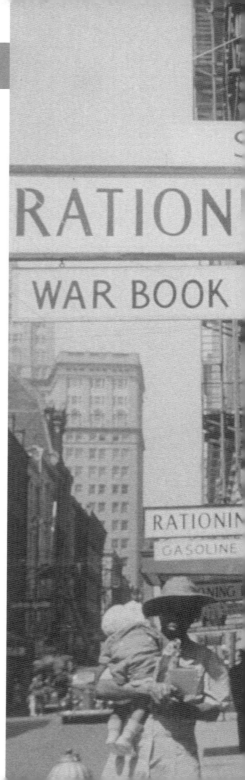

HOES

NG BOARD

WAR BOOK I

BOARD

FIRES

CIVIL DEFENSE: AIR RAID WARDENS

On May 20, 1941, the Civil Defense was started by the Government Office of Emergency Management. The Civil Defense was comprised of a group of volunteers who helped with the protection of fellow civilians, usually their neighbors, during air raids and other emergencies. Each city was responsible for recruiting and organizing its own Civil Defense organization to ensure that it would be able to handle any emergency that arose.

Air raid wardens were key to the Civil Defense. After training, they were given manuals that outlined their duties: direct people to shelters, cooperate with police in directing traffic, control lights in blackouts and dim-outs, report bombs, go to spots of disaster, size up damage and danger, report conditions to a report center, take temporary command to avert panic, render first aid, control fires, account for families, and assist children and the elderly.

While the list of duties was impressive, the main job of the air raid warden was making sure people complied with blackout restrictions. Following the attack on Pearl Harbor in 1941, there were fears of bombing

† A glimpse at an air raid warden meeting.

attacks by Germany as well as the more realistic threat of German U-boats operating in the Atlantic. At the time, aviators didn't use radar to find cities to bomb; they used lights. Blackouts and dim-outs went into effect, requiring that the lights of all houses and neighborhoods be turned off at specified times and black curtains be used on windows.

Journalist Mike Royko described his memory of blackouts and air raid wardens when he was a child:

The siren would go off and everybody would turn off the lights. [The air raid warden] would go around the neighborhood banging on doors yelling, 'Your lights are on.' He'd write down people's names. I didn't like this. My younger brother and I would sit in this pitch-black apartment. We were afraid that if we didn't . . . the FBI would come and terrible things would happen!

✛ Air raid warden posters were used to entice people to volunteer for the positions.

CONSCRIPTION: THE DRAFT

Before World War II, most Americans didn't travel beyond their home-towns, let alone out of the country. In 1941, that changed. New legislation made military service mandatory for most men, and suddenly they were shipping out to places they'd never even heard of. More than 12 million men were drafted during WWII, more than during the First World War, the Korean War, and the Vietnam War combined.

A peacetime draft law was put into effect in September 1940, which required all men between the ages of 21 and 36 living in the United States to register for the draft. Under the law, during peacetime, no more than 900,000 men could be drafted by the government; the law also said soldiers could not be sent overseas.

After the bombing of Pearl Harbor, these laws changed like everything else. The minimum age was changed from 21 to 20; then in 1943, it was lowered to 18. Also, the military could draft an unlimited number of men. Initially, men could volunteer before being drafted, which meant that they could choose the branch of service they went into: army, navy, or Marines. In 1943, the law was amended again, and men were not allowed to volunteer but had to go to the branch the government chose for them.

The wartime draft law differed from the peacetime law in another important way. The government could now send enlisted men anywhere in the world. Suddenly, boys who'd never left Kalamazoo, Michigan, or Tuscaloosa, Alabama, found themselves en route to exotic or not-so-exotic locations in Europe, Asia, Africa, or South America.

President Franklin D. Roosevelt opens the first selective service lottery, October 15, 1940.

DOMESTIC TRAVEL

Not everyone who traveled left the country with the armed forces. With the improved economy, people now left their hometowns in search of better jobs and living environments. For instance, residents of a steel town no longer felt confined to working at the local steel mill. The flowing

economy gave people the hopes and dreams that had eluded them during the Great Depression. And they left home to follow those dreams.

During World War II, more than 15 million civilians moved to a new residence; more than half of them moved out of their home state. This mass resettlement was far greater than the westward expansion that took place during the 1800s.

This internal migration had a profound effect on the way Americans viewed one another. Different types of people met for the first time and were able to gain understanding about one another. City dwellers met country folks, Northerners met Southerners, and minorities became more familiar to the larger population. In the best cases, tolerance for one another grew. In the worst cases, racism flourished.

JAPANESE RELOCATION CENTERS

A mere 74 days after Pearl Harbor, Japanese Americans became the victims of Executive Order No. 9066. In response to the fear that they may be undercover agents for Japan, President Roosevelt issued an order that forced more than 110,000 Japanese Americans to leave their homes in states that included California, Washington, and Oregon and live in one of 10 detention camps scattered across the United States.

Two-thirds of these Japanese Americans, called *Nisei* or second generation, had been born in the United States. None of them had committed or been charged with any crime against the government. Still, they were suspects and guilty until proven innocent.

The government called these camps "relocation centers." Surrounded by barbed wire and armed guards, families survived in overcrowded barracks. The barracks had no running water, little heat, and no privacy.

One of those interned was Norman Mineta, who later became secretary of commerce under President Clinton and secretary of transportation under President George W. Bush.

We had just come home from being at a church service at the Japanese Methodist Church in San Jose, California. I heard the news reports about the Japanese attacking the U.S. naval facility. I've seen my dad cry three times. Once on the seventh of December. He was an immigrant, as was

Japanese Americans in Los Angeles boarding trains for relocation centers, 1942.

my mother, from Japan. He couldn't understand how the land of his birth was attacking the land of his heart. The second was on the 29th of May 1942, the day we boarded the trains under military guard as we were being shipped off to camp. The third time was when my mother died.

Mineta was a driving force behind the Civil Liberties Act of 1988, which gave each internee $20,000 from the U.S. government and an apology that listed as the causes of the internment camps "race prejudice, war hysteria, and a failure of political leadership. Widespread ignorance of Japanese Americans contributed to a policy conceived in haste and executed in an atmosphere of fear and anger at Japan."

This fear continued through most of World War II. Even when it was clear that Japan was losing the war, most of the Japanese Americans were kept in camps well into 1944. The last camp did not close until March 1946, seven months after the war had ended.

⊬ A Japanese-American business owner placed a sign in his window identifying himself as an American on December 8, 1941.

⊬ Ansel Adams photo of the noon mess line at the Manzanar, California, relocation camp for Japanese Americans.

JIM CROW AT HOME AND ABROAD

While American troops were losing their lives fighting against Hitler's horrendous racism, Americans maintained a segregated army and a legal system of discrimination against African Americans at home.

Jim Crow laws, which were named after a popular minstrel-show character and which kept African Americans "separate but equal" from whites, thrived in the southern states. And though people were usually separate, conditions were rarely equal. The signs over many bathrooms, restaurants, drinking fountains, and other facilities instructed COLORED ONLY or WHITE ONLY. African Americans could be drafted, but they rarely had a say in government policy. When they could find jobs, they were generally the last to be hired, the first to be fired, and, along with women, the lowest paid.

Due to the needs of the war, some of these situations changed. With so much of the workforce being drafted and

(opposite): An African-American worker manufactures casings for 105mm shells in Detroit, Michigan, January 1943.

"above and beyond the call of duty"

DORIE MILLER
*Received the Navy Cross
at Pearl Harbor, May 27, 1942*

Dorie Miller received the Navy Cross for his heroism at Pearl Harbor.

✈ African-American recruits training in Illinois.

shipped overseas, and the war industry flourishing, workers were hired regardless of their sex or color.

The discrimination was the same or worse in the army. German prisoners of war were sometimes treated more fairly than African-American soldiers. African Americans could enlist but were usually put in non-combat supply and service jobs. The government was of the opinion that African Americans could not fight.

African American Doris "Dorie" Miller enlisted in the U.S. Navy as a mess attendant, third class. In September 1939, he was promoted to ship's cook, third class, and was serving on the battleship USS *West Virginia* when the Japanese attacked Pearl Harbor on December 7, 1941. After saving an officer, Miller manned an anti-aircraft machine gun until he ran out of ammunition and was ordered to abandon ship. Of his experience fighting against the barrage of Japanese planes, he said, "It wasn't hard. I just pulled the trigger, and she worked fine. I had watched the others with these guns. I guess I fired her for about 15 minutes. I think I got one of those Japanese planes. They were diving pretty close to us."

On May 27, 1942, Fleet Admiral Chester Nimitz, the commander of the Pacific Fleet, personally presented Miller with the Navy Cross for his extraordinary courage in battle. Many felt he deserved the Medal of Honor, the highest award.

On November 24, 1943, Dorie Miller was killed when the ship he was stationed aboard, the USS *Liscome Bay*, was hit by a Japanese torpedo.

WOMEN IN THE WAR: ROSIE THE RIVETER

The war brought about great change for men shipped off to battle, but in some ways, the changes were greater for women at home. As more and more men left to fight, women began taking over traditionally male responsibilities, inside the home and outside. Suddenly, women who had been confined to their roles as homemaker, mother, and wife were able to work outside the home. Not only was it socially acceptable now to get a job out of the home, but it was also applauded.

The Rosie the Riveter character was originally a *Saturday Evening Post* cover illustration created by Norman Rockwell. His Rosie is a brawny yet innocent-looking woman in overalls, cradling her rivet gun in her lap, goggles pushed up onto her forehead, and holding a sandwich. That name was later given to a kerchief-wearing, muscle-flexing woman featured in a popular poster under the credo "We Can Do It!" This poster served as a morale booster for the many women entering the workforce.

More than six million American women became war workers in factories. They helped assemble bombs, build tanks, weld hulls, and

The poster with the slogan "We Can Do It!" served as a morale booster for women who became factory war workers.

grease locomotives. A popular song of the day praised Rosie the Riveter in verse:

All the day long, whether rain or shine, she's a part of the assembly line.
She's making history, working for victory, Rosie the Riveter.
Keeps a sharp lookout for sabotage, sitting up there on the fuselage.
That little girl will do more than a male will do.
Rosie's got a boyfriend, Charlie. Charlie, he's a Marine.
Rosie is protecting Charlie, working overtime on the riveting machine.
When they gave her a production 'E,' she was as proud as she could be.
There's something true about, red, white, and blue about, Rosie the Riveter.

⊢ A real-life Rosie the Riveter works on the construction of a Liberty ship.

Though considered by many to be better at some factory tasks than men, most women were paid only 60 percent of men's wages. And though the work provided some financial independence, many women faced harassment on the job. Plus, those women with children were one of the first generations to have to juggle the roles of mother and breadwinner. Few commanded as much respect as men, not even from the government who requested their services. "A woman is a substitute," claimed a War Department brochure, "like plastic instead of metal."

But this experience in the workforce erased a lot of the social stigmas for working women, opening up a world of opportunity.

WOMEN JOURNALISTS

The war expanded professional opportunities for all women, including women who already had careers. Female journalists were no exception. They fought for and won the right to cover the biggest story of the time, World War II. By war's end, at least 127 American women had official military accreditation as war correspondents. Other women journalists remained in America and documented the ways in which the war affected the home front.

Janet Flanner

American-born Janet Flanner wrote about World War II for the *New Yorker* magazine. She also did a weekly radio broadcast for NBC. She was known for sensitive work about the war's implications for the future of European civilization.

While covering the Nuremberg trials, she wrote:

When you look at the startling ruins of Nuremberg, you are looking at a result of the war. When you look at the prisoners on view in the courthouse, you are looking at 22 of the causes.

Clare Boothe Luce

Clare Boothe Luce is well known as a congress-woman, an ambassador, a playwright, and the wife of Henry Luce, the publisher and founder of *Time* and *Life* magazines. What many people don't know is that Luce covered a wide range of World War II battlefronts as a writer. A beautiful socialite, Luce behaved like a seasoned

Janet Flanner conversing with Ernest Hemingway.

＋ Dwight D. Eisenhower meets with Clare Boothe Luce.

war reporter, suffering bombing raids and many other discomforts.

Her observations of Italy, France, Belgium, the Netherlands, and England in the midst of the German campaigns were published in 1940 in a book called *Europe in the Spring*.

Throughout the war, Luce would be where the action was, interviewing dignitaries such as Jawaharlal Nehru, China's Supreme Commander Chiang Kai-shek, and General "Vinegar Joe" Stilwell, the commander of American troops in the China-Burma-India theater.

Therese Bonney

Photographer Therese Bonney chronicled the civilian victims of World War II, including homeless children and adults on the back roads of Europe. Bonney was educated in the United States and moved to France in the 1920s. Going on what she called "truth raids," Bonney would travel without protection into the countryside to record the horror of war. Bonney said, "I go forth alone, try to get the truth and then bring it back and try to make others face it and do something about it."

Bonney was also the subject of a World War II comic book called *Photo-fighter*, which included quite non-comical topics.

May Craig

When not in Washington, D.C., producing her column for Gannett newspapers, May Craig was providing eyewitness accounts of the Normandy campaign, the liberation of Paris, and V-bomb raids of London.

Craig, a former suffragist, also organized numerous programs to raise the professional status of female news correspondents. Although she single-handedly overturned more than one military rule designed to keep women out of planes and off of ships, even she could not always convince male officials that women could rough it if required.

WOMEN IN THE RANKS: WACS, WAVES, WASPS...

Early in 1941, Massachusetts Congresswoman Edith Rogers told the army's chief of staff, General George C. Marshall, that she intended to introduce a bill to establish a women's corps in the army.

Although revolutionary, it wasn't that far-fetched. During World War I, women volunteers worked overseas with the army as communications specialists and dietitians. Unfortunately, they had no official status, which meant they received no legal protection or medical care and were not entitled to pensions or disability insurance. They even had to obtain their own food and living quarters! The new bill Congresswoman Rogers proposed would provide women with the same benefits as men in the army.

Although the government understood the need, the bill didn't really catch on until after the bombing of Pearl Harbor, when lawmakers saw the great need for women's support in the ranks. With the United States fighting a war on two fronts, the Pacific and Europe, the more able bodies the country had, the better its chances of winning.

The government began a spirited ad campaign to convince women to take the place of men in noncombat positions in the army. With women in clerical and telephone-operator jobs, men would be freed up to go into battle and defeat the enemy.

⊢ A formation of WACs (Women's Army Corps) in Italy, 1945.

On May 14, 1942, the Women's Army Auxiliary Corps (WAAC) was established. Officers and enlisted women were given appointments comparable, but not identical, to those held by men in the army. At first, WAACs (which became WACs) received less pay than their male counterparts, but on November 1, 1942, they began to get the same pay and allowances as members of the regular army.

WAVES, or Women Accepted for Volunteer Emergency Service, the Women's Reserve of the U.S. Naval Reserve, was established later in 1942. WAVES' role was similar to that of the WACs' except they were trained for shore duty, thus releasing men for combat duty at sea.

The Women Airforce Service Pilots, or WASPs, began on August 5, 1943. WASPs flew B-29 Superfortress bombers, P-51 Mustang fighter planes, and the first American military jet planes. Although they ferried aircraft from factories to bases, tested planes, and trained pilots, women were not permitted to fly in combat. WASP pilots did not have military status, although the commanding general of the Army Air Force, Henry "Hap" Arnold, said, "If there was a doubt in anyone's mind that women can become skillful pilots, the WASPs have dispelled that doubt."

The Coast Guard had a female reserve as well, which began in 1942. Women in the Coast Guard were known as SPARs, a name derived from the Coast Guard motto, "*Semper Paratus—Always Ready.*" As with the WAVES, SPARs were enlisted and trained for shore duty, releasing the men to fight at sea.

Although the Marine Corps Women's Reserve members were the first to wear the forest-green uniform with the globe-and-anchor insignia in World War I, they were not officially recognized until February 13, 1943. Like the WAVES and the SPARs, the Women's Reserve was organized to replace men of

⊢ The Women's Army Auxiliary Corps used posters such as this to recruit new members.

✠ A group of Women Airforce Service Pilots leaves the operations hanger, preparing to board for a routine flight.

the Marine Corps for noncombat duties. Unlike the WAC, WAVES, and SPARs, these women had no official nickname but were known as WRs. They became WMs, or Women Marines, in June 1948, when President Truman signed the Women's Armed Services Integration Act, which allowed the enlistment and appointment of women in the regular navy and the regular Marine Corps.

HOW PEOPLE GOT THE NEWS

During World War II, newspapers were one of the few ways to find out what was happening overseas. With no television or Internet, people read papers to find news and see photos and detailed maps of combat theaters, which helped Americans figure out exactly where fighting occurred.

Though Americans received much of the news of the war from their early newspapers, radio broadcasts brought the war into their homes in a whole new way. Nearly every family had a radio that was tuned in for the latest dispatches.

Radio carried the war action from Europe and the Pacific, and the war correspondents became familiar, reassuring voices. The most famous correspondent was Edward R. Murrow. Broadcasting nightly from London in 1940, his descriptions of the Blitz, the German bombing raids, gave firsthand accounts with an immediacy one could not get from a newspaper. Here is an excerpt:

Tonight, as on every other night, the 'rooftop watchers' are peering out across the fantastic forest of London's chimney pots. The anti-aircraft gunners stand ready. . . . I have been walking tonight—there is a full moon, and the dirty-gray buildings appear white. The stars, the empty windows, are hidden. It's a beautiful and lonesome city where men and women and children are trying to snatch a few hours' sleep underground.

 Insider's view of the West End London subway station that doubled as an air raid shelter.

War correspondents landed along with the troops and covered the war throughout Europe and the Pacific. Americans were informed of everything from MacArthur's return to the Philippines to the dropping of atomic bombs on Hiroshima and Nagasaki. People were also able to hear excerpts of speeches by Hitler, Mussolini, and Churchill, and weekly addresses by President Roosevelt, known as Fireside Chats.

American moviegoers were kept up to date about events at home and on the war fronts by twice-weekly newsreels, short films that were shown before movies or in between double features. Newsreels looked very much like news broadcasts but without anchor people. Visual images of combat, basic training, and the decorating of war heroes were narrated by an announcer. With footage that included the devastation at Pearl Harbor and in England, newsreels brought the war to life and Americans strongly behind the nation.

PROPAGANDA

While World War II was being fought on the front lines with warplanes, troops, and aircraft carriers, another weapon was hard at work at home—propaganda, the intentional spreading of information to further one's cause. All governments attempted to sway the hearts and minds of their citizens through the use of posters, leaflets, brochures, films, and radio broadcasts.

The Nazis showed films comparing Jews to rats that needed to be exterminated. The Italians used propaganda to make their lost battles sound like victories. And Japanese propaganda posters pictured the Japanese chopping their way through the fields of humanity.

United States propaganda messages had varying motives. Some were used to promote patriotism and pride in America. Posters showed soldiers or women workers and had slogans like "America Will Always Fight" and "We Can Do It!" Others advertised particular military branches—"U.S. Navy: It Takes a Man!" or "U.S. Army Air Force: Coming Right Up!"—or the need for people to purchase war bonds. There were posters that instructed people to plant victory gardens, ration goods, and repair their clothes instead of buying new ones. There was a chilling message to carpool that said: "When You Ride Alone, You Ride With Hitler."

Some posters were created to inspire fear of the enemy. People tend to be strongly behind a war effort if they feel they are in danger. The images were grim,

This is just one sample of the propaganda used to motivate people to support the war.

 Hollywood movie star and "pin-up" girl Rita Hayworth pictured "harvesting a bumper crop for Uncle Sam."

PLEASE DRIVE CAREFULLY. MY BUMPERS ARE ON THE SCRAP HEAP

sinister, and sometimes scary, portraying the war's hazards and villains. They showed Japanese soldiers looking like sneaky brutish animals or Germans with long claws trying to steal little babies from the arms of moms. Others warned, "Loose Lips Sink Ships," against telling secrets about the war.

Hollywood movies sometimes assisted in spreading the message. The plot points were pretty simple: Bad guys were bad, good guys were good, and America was great. There were movies that were battle-related, such as *Bataan* (1943) and *Guadalcanal Diary* (1943). Others movies were fictitious illustrations of what war life was like, such as *Mrs. Miniver* (1942), about England during the London Blitz, and *Casablanca* (1942), about the Nazis and the French Resistance in Morocco. There were even war comedies, such as *Hail the Conquering Hero* (1944), about a guy who, after being told he is ineligible for the Marines, fakes his heroic career.

At its best, the use of propaganda in America underscored traditional values and the "just cause" of the war.

VICTORY

When the war finally came to an end (May 8, 1945, in Europe and August 15, 1945, in the Pacific), victory was declared by the Allies, but there were enormous losses as well.

America suffered fewer fatalities than other nations, but the numbers were still heartbreaking. Although an exact number is not known, it is estimated that there were 300,000 deaths out of 16 million American uniformed men and women. The Soviet Union had the greatest loss with 21.3 million casualties, while China suffered 11.3 million. In Germany, more than seven million people died.

In the last year of the war, the Allies suffered the sad loss of the president who guided the United States through the war. Franklin Delano Roosevelt died on April 12, 1945, from a massive cerebral hemorrhage. He was replaced by his vice president, Harry S Truman. Roosevelt would miss the victory in Europe by less than a month, and the nation would miss him long after.

⊬ Times Square celebrates the signing of the armistice. Although the signing was just a rumor, New Yorkers continued to celebrate.

For the United States, victory meant the war was over and "our boys" would be coming home, but there were other victories as well. The economy was booming, Americans were back to work, patriotism was high, the country was moving in the right direction, and for the first time in a long time, there was hope for the future.

Although there was great sadness for the lives that had been lost, people still celebrated the return of their loved ones. More than 500,000 people crammed into Times Square in New York City chanting, "It's over! It's over!" Across the nation, cities and towns filled with merry-makers who jitterbugged, hugged, kissed, sang, laughed, and cried. Car horns honked, confetti flew, sirens wailed, and church bells rang. Factories closed early, and store owners shut their doors and hung signs that said CLOSED FOR PEACE. And for a time, there was peace.

New York celebrates America's victory over Japan in Times Square.

GLOSSARY

Allies—The name for the nations, primarily Great Britain, the United States, the Soviet Union, and France, united against the Axis powers.

Atomic Bomb—An explosive weapon made of either uranium or plutonium that gets its destructive power from the rapid release of nuclear energy.

Axis—The countries, primarily Germany, Italy, and Japan, that fought against the Allies.

Campaign—A series of major military operations designed to achieve a long-range goal.

Capitulation—An agreement of surrender.

Dignitaries—Anyone of high rank.

Fireside Chats—The informal name for President Franklin Roosevelt's radio speeches to the American people that updated them on important events of the day.

Internment—The detaining or confining of individuals in wartime. Usually done by a neutral country when combatants enter its boundaries.

Nazi—The acronym for NAtionalsoZIalist, the first word of the official title of Hitler's political party, the Nationalsozialistische Deutsche Arbeiterpartie or NSDAP (National Socialist German Workers' Party).

Nisei—Native born, second-generation Japanese-American citizens.

Resistance—An underground organization engaged in the struggle for national liberation in a country under military occupation.

Sabotage—The damage of property or actions of a country by enemy spies.

Soviet Union—From 1917–1991, the nation known officially as the Union of Soviet Socialist Republics; a nation containing 15 communist-governed republics and dominated by its largest republic, Russia.

Theater—The large geographical area where military operations are coordinated.

U-Boat—Abbreviation for the German term *Unterseeboot* (underwater boat). The name commonly given German submarines.

INDEX